To Bakari,
1999
From Your Loving Link

NEVER GIVE UP

The Marshall Jones Story

by

Cheryl A. Weinstein

Perennial Press
Glenville, New York

Copyright © 1999 M.G. Jones and C.A. Weinstein. Printed and bound in the United States of America. All rights reserved. No part of this book may be reproduced or transmitted in any form or by any means, electronic or mechanical, including photocopying, recording, or by an information storage and retrieval system, without permission in writing from the publisher.

For more information, please contact Perennial Press, P.O. Box 2837, Glenville, NY 12325-0837. First printing 1999.

ISBN 0-9670317-0-2

Library of Congress Catalog Card Number: 99-94096

Acknowledgments

We would like to express our appreciation to Patricia Henderson's 1995 fourth grade class at the Zoller Elementary School in Schenectady, New York. The students who critiqued the story draft provided insightful comments and suggestions, many of which were incorporated into the final version.

We would also like to thank our families and friends for all their support during this endeavor.

Especially For Mom -

*Your unending love and support have
inspired me to do things I never thought possible;
To reach for the stars - and
Never Give Up.*

CHAPTER 1

Eight-year-old Marshall sat on the porch step, sweat running down his dirty face. His dog Friskie flopped down next to him, dropping a slimy baseball from his mouth. Marshall looked at him and smiled. He knew Friskie wanted to play catch, but he was too tired today. He had been herding those ducks into the main building for what felt like days! Uncle Lawrence had asked him to make sure all the ducks were inside, safe and dry for the night. It was peak season, and there were at least 80,000 ducks on the ranch. Marshall was exhausted! Finally, he was beginning to realize what his uncle had always told him was the truth. The duck ranch was definitely hard work!

Poor Uncle Lawrence, Marshall thought. He works such long hours, day and night, seven days a week, and does not make much money at all. Suddenly he could hear his uncle's words ringing in his

Never Give Up

ears: *When you grow up, work with your mind, not just your hands. Do the best you can in school. Then you will be successful and have a good life.*

Marshall thought about this for a long time. His uncle had repeated those words to him many times. He was finally beginning to truly understand. Marshall now made a promise to himself. When he grew up, he was not going to work 80 hours a week on the duck ranch like Uncle Lawrence. No way. The jet planes overhead interrupted his thoughts, and he looked up.

Maybe I'll be a pilot, he thought. That would be really neat. You must have to use math and science to fly a plane. Those were his best subjects, not like English, where he always had so much trouble. And how he loved to listen to all the flying adventures of "Sky King" on the radio! Why, he never missed that program unless he absolutely could not help it. Marshall was now very excited. That was IT! He was going to be a pilot, just like Sky King. He leaped to his feet and raced down the steps of the porch, Friskie nipping playfully at his heels. He had to find Uncle Lawrence and tell him the exciting news!

Marshall, age 8, with Friskie on duck ranch.

Never Give Up

Marshall's mother Mildred in front of house (Marshall's second home) on duck ranch.

CHAPTER 2

Marshall Gordon Jones was born on August 1, 1941, at Southhampton Hospital, on Eastern Long Island, in New York State. Before he was born, his mother, Mildred Jones, had been certain her baby would be a girl. Her name would be Sarah Antoinette. Of course, when her baby turned out to be a boy, Mildred Jones knew she could not call him Sarah! She had to think of a new name - and fast. So she began thinking of her baby's family. She decided on Marshall as the baby's first name, after her own grandfather, Marshall Jackson. Gordon would be the baby's middle name, after his grandfather, James Gordon Jones. So, Sarah Antoinette Jones became Marshall Gordon Jones, his mother's first-born.

When Mildred and her son left Southhampton Hospital, they went to live with Mildred's Uncle

Never Give Up

Lawrence and Aunt Mary in the tiny farming village of Aquebogue (pronounced Ack-qua-borg). Although Aquebogue was on Long Island, it was nothing like the big city. In the 1940s, the population was only about 900. In fact, in the whole village, there was only one traffic light - and a blinking one at that!

It was during World War II, and Marshall's father, Dallas Jones, was in the Navy, far away from Aquebogue. He was rarely able to come home on leave. Mildred worked on the Cowen Duck Ranch with Uncle Lawrence and Aunt Mary. They all lived together in a small one-story house (Marshall's first home), just 50 yards from the duck processing plant.

Although Mildred Jones still hoped for a baby girl, it was not to be. One year later she had her second child, who also turned out to be a boy, named Melvin. But she loved her sons a great deal.

For the first two years of his life, Mildred would braid little Marshall's hair. He could tell this made his mother happy, so Marshall was happy too. He loved his mother so much. Indeed, he was a carefree, content baby, living on the ranch, during his early years.

Marshall with braids, age 2.

Uncle Lawrence

Aunt Mary

CHAPTER 3

By the time Marshall turned 2, Mildred Jones had begun to worry about him. He had long since started to talk, but no one could understand a word he said. No one except his baby brother Melvin and the family dog.

Mildred decided to take Marshall to the doctor. There they discovered that he had been born tongue-tied. This happens when the web underneath the newborn's tongue has not been broken. Doctors usually check this at birth, but in Marshall's case, his doctor had not done it.

So Marshall had an operation where the doctor clipped the web under his tongue. This corrected the medical problem. But now Marshall had to learn to talk again.

All of the earlier time he had spent learning to

Never Give Up

speak was lost. He had to start over. He did not completely understand what was happening and grew impatient when his tongue now thrashed about, out of control, whenever he tried to speak.

Although he was still quite young, he felt self-conscious about this. The experience would stay with him for many years to come.

*   *   *

When Marshall was almost 4 years old, Mildred Jones went away to New York City to find a better job. Marshall loved his mother dearly and did not want her to go. But she promised she would be coming back often to visit.

These visits were like a roller coaster ride for Marshall. When his mother came home, he would be very happy. She always looked so beautiful and was dressed in such elegant clothes. He loved to have her home. But time flew by much too fast. Soon she would have to walk to the station, just 100 yards away from their house, to catch the train for New York City again.

In his mind, Marshall knew the ride was not that long. They had told him that. New York City was only

83 miles from Aquebogue. But, in his young heart, it seemed like a million miles away. And anyway, weren't mothers supposed to stay home with their children? Why did she have to always leave him? Each time she boarded the train, he would cry so hard, long after she was gone. He thought his heart would break into tiny pieces and fall all over the ground.

But Uncle Lawrence and Aunt Mary were always there to comfort Marshall and his younger brother. They tried to tell the boys that their mother loved them very much. They encouraged the boys to talk about their sadness, which they did. Knowing Uncle Lawrence and Aunt Mary were there to love and take care of them somehow always made things better.

Mildred dressed in her elegant clothes.

CHAPTER 4

Aquebogue Elementary School went from first through eighth grade. There was no kindergarten. At age 5, Marshall reluctantly started school as a first-grade student. It was a terribly traumatic experience for him. His shyness went deep, and the whole idea of school frightened him a great deal. He was so scared he could not even bring himself to ask the teacher if he could use the bathroom.

After two weeks, it was decided that Marshall would begin school the following September instead, when he would be 6 years old. So, much to his relief, he returned home to spend his days on the ranch, in comforting, familiar surroundings once again. He did not want to even think about school anymore. He did not care if he ever went back there!

Of course, the following September did come,

Never Give Up

and 6-year-old Marshall found himself back in the first grade. This time, though, it was somewhat better. He was still shy, but being one year older did make a difference.

*   *   *

One of the worst things about school in Marshall's mind was reading. He was not a good reader. In fact, he thought he was a total failure when it came to reading. He had not really read books before he began school. The family sang hymns on Saturday nights, and he did read from the hymnal. But he already knew those words by heart. This was the extent of his reading experiences prior to starting the first grade.

Marshall totally dreaded days when the teacher went around the room asking each child to read. Although he liked Mrs. Rackett immensely, he did not like this reading exercise she forced on the class. Marshall would sink deeper and deeper in his seat, thinking maybe that would help him to escape the terrible fate. Maybe she would not notice him.

But it always came. His turn to read. He knew he was not a good reader. He was too slow. And knowing made it that much worse. He would feel hot waves flash over his entire body. His mouth would go dry. When he started to speak, his voice would shake. He just knew everyone was making fun of him, however quiet they seemed. Oh, how he dreaded those days.

Spelling bees were another punishment worse than death for Marshall. His spelling was not much better than his reading. The English language appeared to give him trouble from every direction! He never wanted to be on any spelling bee team, because he knew he would let them down, no matter how hard he tried.

The shy, insecure feelings kept coming back to haunt Marshall over and over. He began to wonder if he would ever gain any confidence in his lifetime.

Never Give Up

Marshall at age 6.

CHAPTER 5

Things began to change for Marshall in the second grade. He found one subject he really loved. The subject was arithmetic, and it surprised him to learn he was quite good with numbers.

He also found other positive things about school. His second grade teacher, Mrs. Hallock, was the youngest - and prettiest - teacher Marshall had ever known. Mrs. Hallock introduced two new subjects to her class. They were penmanship and art. Both appealed to Marshall. He liked the feeling of creating something with his hands.

There was one more thing he now really liked about school. That was recess.

Marshall was an athletic boy. His coordination skills were excellent. He enjoyed baseball the most. He also liked square dancing. The class would form

Never Give Up

squares in the basement of the school when the weather did not permit the students to go outside to play. Each group wanted Marshall in their square because he was such a good dancer. This made him happy and also helped raise his confidence a bit.

Marshall continued to have difficulty with his reading, which began to affect other areas of his studies. Tests were a real problem. Because of his slow reading, he would often run out of time before he could answer all the questions. In arithmetic, though, he only got better.

By third grade, Marshall was doing sixth grade math. He loved the subject and the pride that came with doing well in something. Uncle Lawrence and Aunt Mary, who had only completed second and third grades, were also very proud of their great-nephew's accomplishments.

Marshall's hopes and goals were now coming into focus in his young mind. He watched all the television shows about World War II, with the planes and battleships. He listened to the adventures of the pilot "Sky King" on the radio. In art class, he drew detailed pictures of planes. And he dreamed of one day becoming a pilot.

Just when Marshall thought things were looking

up, his third grade teacher, Mrs. Edwards, came up with a new idea. She began to tape record each student as he or she read. Marshall had not gotten over his shyness at reading aloud. In his eyes, the tape recorder only made a bad situation much, much worse. The machine was his enemy. To hear, with his own ears, all his mistakes, replayed for the whole class, was almost unbearable.

Uncle Lawrence continuously tried to encourage Marshall to use his mind. He wanted so much for both boys to succeed. So he devised a numbers game, which Marshall loved.

Every week, Uncle Lawrence, Marshall and Melvin went to the market and tried to add, in their heads, the prices of all the groceries they put into the shopping cart. Then, when they reached the checkout line, they each tried to guess the total amount of the bill. The one who came closest to the correct amount won. Marshall was always the winner!

How Marshall loved the numbers game. But he loved his uncle even more, for he knew it was his way of caring, trying to encourage them and to make learning fun.

Never Give Up

AQUEBOGUE ELEMENTARY SCHOOL
A. L. Edgar, Principal
REPORT TO PARENTS

Name *Marshall Jones* Grade *2*
Date *January 31* to *April 8*

Geography	
Arithmetic	A
Spelling	D
Reading, Silent	D
Reading, Oral	D+
English	
History	
Writing	A
Drawing	B
Science	
Social Studies	

COMMENTS

Marshall shows progress in his work as his interest grows. He needs to work hard at his reading. As his reading improves his spelling will too.

Mrs. Hallock, Teacher

CODE

A—Excellent 90-100
B—Good 80-90
C—Average 70-80
D—Poor 60-70
F—Failure less than 60

ATTENDANCE
Days Absent 9 Times Tardy —

Marshall's report card, grade 2.

CHAPTER 6

Fourth grade became a real struggle for Marshall. Although he had grown to like school in many ways, English continued to haunt him. It was by far his worst subject, and his reading skills were not improving. He had been passed to fourth grade only because of his advanced skills in math.

One day, near the end of the school year, Aunt Mary was called in to meet with Marshall's teacher, Mrs. DeFriest, who was deeply concerned about her student. After a long discussion, they decided it would be best for Marshall to repeat fourth grade. Hopefully, with more study and practice, he could catch up and become a better reader.

At first, Marshall was shocked to learn that he was not going into fifth grade with his fellow students. He was afraid they might make fun of him, and

Never Give Up

he would not have any friends. But this was not the case at all.

Repeating fourth grade made all the difference in the world to Marshall. His reading did improve. This also gave him more confidence in himself and his abilities. In the end, he was very glad he had stayed back. In his mind, it had changed his life.

During this time, Marshall continued to be active in sports. He still loved art, especially drawing. He also loved music. He played the brass cymbals in the school band and sang in the school choir. When his voice changed, he left the school choir. Later he joined the junior choir at the First Baptist Church and became more involved in activities there.

The strong religious beliefs Marshall learned from the First Baptist Church, and from his family, taught him to care more about other people. These beliefs deeply influenced him and would contribute a great deal to the adult Marshall Gordon Jones would become.

Mrs. DeFriest's grade 4 class
(Marshall, top row, third from left).

Marshall's report card, repeated grade 4.

CHAPTER 7

That summer, when Marshall was 10, he and Melvin began to spend summer vacations with their mother in Springfield, Massachusetts. Mildred missed her children and wanted to spend time with them. She had moved from New York City and was working as a seamstress for a large company named Carter's. She and Dallas Jones had divorced, and she was engaged to marry a man named Harold Bartlett. Mildred had known Harold in Aquebogue. In fact, they had been friends for years. Harold was now also working in Springfield.

Springfield seemed like a big city to the boys. Marshall always felt torn between visiting Mildred and leaving the ranch. He did like to see his mother. He still missed her, although he was more used to her being gone now. But Aquebogue and the duck ranch were his real home, and they always would be. He missed his Aunt Mary and, especially, his Uncle Lawrence during the visits to Springfield.

The boys found there was much to do in the city while visiting. There were many sporting activities, which Marshall enjoyed. There were many movie theaters. Springfield also had a big swimming pool where the boys would spend many hours.

Marshall was not a good swimmer. It was his one athletic weakness. But it was fun to be by the water on those hot summer days.

One afternoon they were at the pool playing a game with three other boys. They were throwing pennies into the water and jumping in to retrieve them.

As they played, Marshall happened to look across the pool and spotted a boy pounce on top of another boy. He was holding him underwater, and the boy could not breathe. For some reason, the lifeguard was not paying attention. He did not see what was happening! Without thinking about his lack of ability, Marshall did the only thing he could do. He dived in, swam frantically across the pool to the mean boy, and hit him as hard as he could. The boy let go of his victim, and Marshall became the hero of the day.

But all in all, Marshall was continuously homesick during the summer visits to Springfield. To him, there was nothing like being in Aquebogue. It was his comfort zone.

Mildred and Harold

Never Give Up

Marshall in grade 5.

CHAPTER 8

After repeating fourth grade, Marshall was now much more comfortable with school. His confidence level slowly rose. He formed a special bond with Mrs. Wright, his fifth grade teacher, who had also taught his mother when she was a young girl.

Marshall also began enjoying another subject. That subject was science. He was fascinated to hear about enormous dinosaurs which roamed the earth many, many years ago. He loved listening to Mrs. Wright talk about the Glacier Age when everything was covered with ice. It was unbelievable to realize that the world had once been so different.

In sixth grade, the first male teacher, Mr. Brandy, came to Aquebogue Elementary School. He was a good teacher and somewhat of a role model for Marshall.

Seventh grade brought a second male teacher, Mr. Ross, to the school. The students really liked Mr. Ross. He introduced many new things to Aquebogue. Mr. Ross and what he brought to the school quickly became important in Marshall's life.

Prior to this, the school had been limited in their sports activities. Mr. Ross introduced wrestling to the school. They played regulation basketball games. Marshall loved both sports and was very good at them.

Mr. Ross also formed an official baseball team. This had been Marshall's favorite of all sports. Riverhead, the nearest town to Aquebogue, had a Little League team. When he was younger, he had wanted so much to be on it. But because his aunt and uncle worked all day, he never had any way to get to the games so could not play. Now Aquebogue Elementary School had a team, and Marshall was on it!

The team went from school to school, playing other area teams. While visiting, they also got to learn more about Long Island itself. Their team was excellent, and they won the majority of their games. It was great fun. These were school memories Marshall would always treasure.

Sports were not the only new things Mr. Ross

brought to the school. In eighth grade, which he also taught, the popular teacher introduced algebra for the first time. Marshall discovered he loved algebra. It also added a new dimension to his above-average math abilities.

With his growing skills in math and science, Marshall Jones, the pilot, was on his way!

*Marshall and class, grade 7
(Marshall middle row, far right, next to Mr. Ross).*

CHAPTER 9

In September of 1956, 15-year-old Marshall Jones entered Riverhead High School as a freshman student. (Aquebogue did not have a high school, and Riverhead was the nearest one to Marshall's home.) The next four years would be a time of many changes. It would also be a time to grow.

The new students he met wondered where the name "Marshall" had come from. Most of them had never heard it as a name before. They thought he might somehow be a junior law officer or something like that. They knew about the United States Marshal and connected the two. His friends decided to call him "Marsh" instead.

Sports began to play an even bigger role in Marshall's life in high school. In ninth grade, he played football, basketball and baseball. Although he

Never Give Up

continued to love all sports, it was now football that he loved the most.

As a freshman, Marshall took a shop class which he enjoyed very much. English was still his most difficult subject. Math continued to come easy, and he aced the algebra final with a perfect score!

During ninth grade, Marshall realized he was having trouble seeing the blackboard, so he went to have his eyes checked. The doctor told him he was nearsighted. This made Marshall really upset. It was 1956, and pilots did not wear glasses. Although contact lenses had been invented many years earlier, they were not widely used until well into the 1960s. All his life, he had wanted to fly planes when he grew up. Now he sadly realized he could never be a pilot.

He began to think more about this situation. He could be a navigator. But that would be too depressing for him. If he could not be a pilot, he did not want to be the second-in-command either.

Somewhere, through all this thought process, the word "engineer" began to develop in his mind. What was an engineer anyway? The person who drove a train was called an engineer. Why wasn't a pilot an engineer too? He knew there must be some connection to this word. But what? He had never known anyone who was an engineer. He decided to keep this in the back of his mind for now. Instead, he began dreaming of a career in sports, in particular professional football.

Another surprise was in store for Marshall during his freshman year at Riverhead High School. Mildred and Harold Bartlett decided to move back to the house with the boys and Aunt Mary and Uncle Lawrence. Now they were all together. Although it was a bit crowded, there was room for all.

<u>Never Give Up</u>

A shy Marshall with friend Frederica.

CHAPTER 10

Marshall Jones continued his quest for excellence in sports as a sophomore. Basketball was out. Because he had only been a freshman, he had spent the last season sitting on the bench more than playing - and hating every minute of it. He wanted to *play*, not watch. If he could not play, he did not want to be on the team. He also dropped baseball. But he picked up two new sports in their place. These were wrestling and track.

On the academic field, Marshall continued to excel in math and science. Math was his passion, though. He relished everything new he learned about it. Unfortunately, not only English, but now history, gave the sophomore a great deal of trouble. He may have been better if he had more time to study. His sports practices always took some of his study time away. Because he was in training, he would go to bed early. In the end, he failed the New York State regents exams in both subjects. It would now be impossible for him to graduate with a regents diploma, which many colleges required.

What ultimately made the most impact on Marshall as a sophomore was a mechanical drawing course he took. To his surprise, he enjoyed this class immensely and was excellent at mechanical drawing. He found it interesting the way it combined some math with the drawing he had loved as a child - when he had spent many hours drawing elaborate planes and dreamed about becoming a pilot.

Again, he would wonder, just briefly, about where an engineer might fit into this picture.

Marshall's 16th birthday party, at home with Mildred.

Never Give Up

Riverhead High's varsity football, offensive formation; Marshall, grade 11, right end (first on left).

CHAPTER 11

In September of his junior year, Mildred, Harold and the boys moved to another home just a few minutes away from Uncle Lawrence and Aunt Mary. Once more, Marshall experienced that old feeling of being torn between two homes. It was fun being with his mother and step-dad, but he loved Uncle Lawrence and Aunt Mary more than anything and felt most comfortable in his own old room.

One night in January 1959, five months after the family moved, Aunt Mary and Uncle Lawrence stopped by for a visit. They had been working all day on the duck ranch and, in the evening, had gone to visit friends. They were on their way home when they stopped to say hello and make sure everyone was okay. As usual, the whole family was happy to see them. It always reminded Marshall how very much

Never Give Up

he missed his aunt and uncle, and how much they both meant to him. Later that night, in his sleep, Uncle Lawrence died of a sudden heart attack. He was 59 years old.

This event devastated Marshall. He could not believe his beloved uncle was gone. It was the worst thing that had ever happened to him. The only thing that got him through and made it possible to go on with his own life was his religious faith. He came to believe, as he had been taught, that there was a reason for everything, even if it was hard to believe at the time. He realized that, in the end, it was a good thing they had moved away in September. If he had been living at the duck ranch, seeing Uncle Lawrence every day as he used to, he believed he could not have survived this horrible loss.

After the funeral for his uncle, Aunt Mary wanted Marshall to come back to live with her. Instead, the whole family decided to move back. Although it was good to be home again, it would never truly be the same without Uncle Lawrence. Marshall missed him terribly.

CHAPTER 12

While a junior at Riverhead High School, Marshall's wrestling coach, Mr. Stewart, had a meeting with the coach at a college named Rochester Institute of Technology (RIT) in Rochester, New York. During this meeting, Coach Stewart recommended Marshall for a wrestling scholarship to RIT. A scholarship pays part of the college's tuition, which can be very expensive. Colleges award scholarships to students who excel in sports or school work.

Things were now progressing well for Marshall. As long as he kept wrestling at the same high level, he would definitely have a scholarship next year and be on his way to college. This was great news. Marshall now spent hours thinking about becoming a wrestling coach, although he still liked the idea of being a professional football player, too. He had

Never Give Up

played football for three years now, and it continued to be the sport he most enjoyed.

But Marshall was to suffer yet another setback early into his senior year which would affect his future. During wrestling practice, his knee buckled, tearing the ligaments. As a result of this injury, he lost all chances for a scholarship to RIT.

Varsity wrestling team, senior year
(Brother Melvin, manager, first on left, middle row; Coach Stewart last on right of middle row; Marshall fifth from left, last row).

CHAPTER 13

Now Marshall had no idea what would become of him. He had no real direction. His future dreams had once again been shattered. His best friend, Uncle Lawrence, who had guided him the most, was no longer there to help him. His mother had been away for so many years, she did not know much about the areas that interested Marshall. She and Harold knew nothing about the math and mechanical drawing Marshall found so exciting. Even his brother had little interest in the things he liked. He found himself so confused. Here he was a senior. He would soon be graduating. And he had no idea what to do with his life. He felt completely alone. The realization hit him hard - he was now solely responsible for his own future.

Marshall decided to talk to Mr. Schaefer, his

Never Give Up

guidance counselor. He explained what subjects he was good in, as well as what ones he liked the most. He told him his school average, about an 85 at the time. Mr. Schaefer then told Marshall about a program where he would be able to use math and mechanical drawing together.

The program was called mechanical engineering technology, and it was offered at a two-year college named Mohawk Valley Community College in Utica, New York. When Marshall graduated from this college, he would be something called a technician, who would work with, of all things, engineers!

Now, Marshall had never heard of a technician, nor had he known about any community college. But the thought of doing something he loved - mechanical drawing - and using math at the same time really appealed to him. He also liked the idea that it was far enough away that he would feel like he was leaving home, but close enough so he could visit often. Since Uncle Lawrence died, the ranch really had not been the same, and it made Marshall sad sometimes.

Without a scholarship, Marshall knew his family did not have enough money to send him away to college. Fortunately, Mohawk Valley Community

College was not too expensive, and he had saved some money from his summer job on the duck ranch, which would help. He took out a loan for the balance of the cost.

So it was decided. Marshall Jones had finally found a new career path. He would be a technician - whatever that was!

Never Give Up
_____

*Riverhead High School 1960 yearbook
Senior photo, "Marsh" Jones.*

CHAPTER 14

Growing up in Aquebogue, Marshall had led a sheltered life compared to what was going on in larger cities throughout the country. The first time he really experienced discrimination was on the night of his high school graduation.

There had been a party for Marshall and Melvin at a club in Riverhead. One of the guests was a close friend named Bill. After their party, they were going on to Bill's party. His party was at a club outside the next town, Mattituck. When they walked in, the manager came over, acting strange. He then asked Marshall and Melvin to leave! The boys did not really understand what was happening. But the manager had asked them to leave simply because they were black.

Bill became very angry that his friends were not

being allowed into the club. A fight almost broke out between Bill and the manager. Finally, the three boys decided it was not worth it to fight, and they left in disgust.

When Marshall went to Utica that September, he was surprised by another similar experience. He had filled out his application for student housing earlier. There had been no information requested on ethnic background. When he arrived, and the owner of the house saw he was black, she told him he could not stay there.

Now he had no place to go. He contacted the school, who immediately took the rooming house off their list of housing for students and found Marshall another, better place to stay.

These two events, although shocking to Marshall at first, made him really begin to think about his heritage. The more he learned, the more he realized that people like the manager at the club or the owner of the rooming house were not very bright, nor very educated. He decided not to waste his time becoming bitter and worrying about the people in the world like them. He would never let them ruin his concentration on being the best he could be.

CHAPTER 15

At Mohawk Valley Community College, Marshall began to spend more time on studying and less on sports. Studying became his main objective. As a high school student and athlete in training, he had been used to going to bed by 8 p.m., whether his homework was done or not. Now in college, he found himself staying up later to make sure all his assignments were finished.

Once he was in a regular schedule, he found it was not so difficult. He was averaging six hours of sleep a night, which was not too bad. To his surprise, he actually became a much better student. His love of mechanical drawing and math continued to grow stronger. By the end of the first year at MVCC, Marshall had passed English with flying colors. Even more astounding, he had the second highest overall

Never Give Up

average in his class. He could not believe it!

Marshall became really motivated. Finally he was beginning to see his future as a reality. He received a paid co-op assignment for the summer, which would help pay for his second year at MVCC.

A co-op assignment is a full-time job, normally set up between the college and a company, in which a student can learn more about the area he is studying. The job is for a short period of time, usually one semester.

In Marshall's case, his first assignment was right at MVCC, as a professor's assistant. In this role, he learned about things called castings, which are made with molds, and how technicians use them to make metal parts. He also learned a great deal about the field of mechanical engineering technology during this time.

CHAPTER 16

Marshall had rarely seen his father, Dallas Jones, while he was growing up. Although he loved Harold Bartlett like a second father, he now had a better opportunity to get to know Dallas, too. Marshall went home to Aquebogue whenever he could. Driving from Utica, he could easily make a stop in New York City, where Dallas lived. His home was right next to the old Polo Grounds, across the river from Yankee Stadium. Marshall stopped frequently, and the two became closer.

*   *   *

The time Marshall spent at MVCC was extremely busy. For one thing, he was involved in starting up a track team at the college. MVCC had

Never Give Up

never, in the history of the school, had a track team. He also was involved in other activities and clubs.

One of these was the Circle K Club, the two-year school version of Key Club or Kiwanis Club. Circle K did a lot of charity work, such as visiting elderly people in the hospitals and helping those in need. Marshall loved to be involved in these things. It always made him feel good inside.

In August of 1961, just before Marshall's senior year at MVCC was to begin, the Circle K was holding a national convention in Florida. Each of the 50 states was sending representatives to attend. Marshall was chosen as a delegate from New York. This was a wonderful opportunity for him, since he had never been any place in his life, except for Massachusetts and Virginia to visit relatives. He was very excited.

During this time, 1961, there were many problems in the South. There were riots between black and white people. When Marshall arrived at the hotel in Florida, he was surprised to learn that, from all the 50 states, he was the only black student there. He was even more surprised when the hotel manager told him he could not register!

When the other students heard this, they were really upset. The group from the Northeast informed the hotel manager that if Marshall had to leave, they were going to leave too. So, even though he did not register, the hotel manager let him stay.

As before, Marshall refused to let the hotel's policy bother him. He was just thrilled to be in Florida. Even though he could not go on the beach, from the hotel he could see the beautiful blue water and the tall palm trees blowing gently in the breeze. The best part of the trip, though, was meeting the other students.

In later years, Marshall was amused to see members of the New York Mets baseball team staying at that same hotel during their spring training. Many of the players were black. He was thankful times had changed!

Dallas in his U.S. Postal Service uniform.

Never Give Up

Class photo, MVCC.

CHAPTER 17

Even before the start of his senior year at MVCC, Marshall had been looking into a second co-op assignment. The college had contacts all around the Utica area and was ready to set something up for him. But this time Marshall wanted to be closer to home. The whole past year had been a huge growing experience for him. Not only had he become a better student, he also became more confident in his work and himself.

Marshall was especially proud of the work he had done in mechanical drawing. He had all A's in the class. So he decided to take his drawings, put them together so they looked professional, and take them around to companies on Long Island.

One of the companies he visited was the well-known Brookhaven National Laboratory, who hired

Never Give Up

him at a pay rate that was higher than his Aunt Mary's! So, already he was seeing the financial benefits of a college education.

During his co-op at Brookhaven, his title was draftsperson. He worked on mechanical drawings similar to those he had done in school. He was thrilled to be involved with such a famous place. He was also proud that he had been the one to make it possible, despite the obstacles that sometimes got in the way. Although there had been times he had felt sad and worried when bad things had happened, he had never given up hope of someday having that good life Uncle Lawrence had wanted so much for him long ago.

Brookhaven National Laboratory was pleased with Marshall's work during this time. He returned to MVCC in March of 1962, with a promise to begin a new co-op assignment with Brookhaven that summer, after graduation.

CHAPTER 18

Marshall's best friend at MVCC was Jack Fogerty. They shared a room in a local rooming house. They were also taking similar classes, although Jack was enrolled in electrical engineering technology courses, rather than the mechanical engineering technology ones Marshall was taking. Jack had been in the Navy for four years before college. Now he had his future planned. After graduating, he was going to transfer to an engineering school to continue his studies.

Marshall had never heard of anything called "transferring" before. He had thought this would be the end of school for him. He would get his two-year degree from MVCC and go to work as a technician. Now Jack had planted a seed in Marshall's head. As the two talked more, he decided he wanted to go to an engineering school, too.

Never Give Up

So Marshall and Jack applied to four colleges which would not be too expensive. Of the four, the best engineering school was the University of Michigan. To their delight, they were both accepted.

They graduated from MVCC on August 10, 1962. Mildred and Harold were there, with their 5-month-old baby boy, Harold Jr. Of course, Aunt Mary came with them. They all watched proudly as Marshall received his two-year A.A.S. degree.

Although Jack went directly to the University of Michigan to begin the fall semester, Marshall did not yet have enough money. So he went back to another co-op assignment at Brookhaven National Laboratory for five months and saved enough for a half-year of college.

In January of 1963, Marshall Jones began his studies at the University of Michigan, with a new goal: *to become an engineer.*

CHAPTER 19

When Marshall had graduated from Riverhead High School, he had thought his English classes were behind him. To his dismay, that was not the case. English was not a subject to be taken lightly at either MVCC or the University of Michigan. Marshall learned that, in addition to his engineering courses, English was also a requirement. Both schools believed that being able to communicate well was important to any job in any field.

Although his grades had improved at MVCC, Marshall still struggled with his English classes. The classes were now more difficult at the University of Michigan. He even had to take a poetry class, in which he had to rewrite every poem he wrote! But he did not give up. He got through the classes, with a C average, and his writing and oral skills improved.

Never Give Up

At the University of Michigan, his love for engineering grew even stronger. He realized it was challenging to learn how to solve scientific problems, which is really what engineering is all about.

His classes varied from math and science to design and drawing. He also spent a large amount of time in the laboratory, a hands-on experience which he enjoyed. The University of Michigan was a tough school. He studied hard, and his overall average was now a low B.

Marshall took out another loan for his junior year and returned to Brookhaven for the summer. His job there was challenging and exciting. He worked on equipment called "bubble chambers" used by engineering teams to study matter. At that time, Brookhaven National Laboratory had the largest bubble chamber in the world.

Marshall had gained much experience at Brookhaven National Laboratory. When he returned to school for his junior year, he could easily identify with what he was studying. Since it was similar to the work he had already been doing at Brookhaven, he was now one step ahead in his school work!

CHAPTER 20

For a number of years, Marshall had been serious about a girl back home. He had met Joyce Franklin during his junior year at Riverhead High School. Joyce was an American Indian, living on the Shinnecock Reservation in Southhampton, New York. While Marshall had been a student at MVCC, he had been close enough to go home frequently to see Joyce. But Michigan was much farther away, and there were times when he did not get home for four months or more.

That summer was a wonderful time for Marshall, not only because he loved his work at Brookhaven. He was happy to be closer to home - and to Joyce.

When Marshall returned to the University of Michigan for his junior year, however, it was not all smooth sailing. His mind often wandered to thoughts of Joyce. As a result, he did so poorly in two of his classes that he had to repeat them.

In the summer of 1964, Marshall again returned to Brookhaven, now as an engineering assistant. For the past months at school, he had thought a great deal about his relationship with Joyce. He realized the long-distance relationship was difficult and that his thoughts of her were seriously affecting his school work. When he returned home that summer, Marshall and Joyce broke up. They did, however, stay good friends.

Back at the University of Michigan for his senior year, Marshall now focussed totally on his studies. He worked harder than he ever had before. By the end of the year, he had brought his overall average back up to a B.

On May 1, 1965, Marshall Gordon Jones graduated from the University of Michigan. Because the class was so large, the ceremony was held in their football stadium, which is the largest stadium in the country. As each department was called, the students rose. When they announced the mechanical engineering department, Marshall stood up proudly with his fellow students. He had made it! He was now officially an engineer.

Before sitting down again, he looked up towards the clear blue sky. He could feel Uncle Lawrence's presence. Marshall knew his uncle would have been very proud.

University of Michigan, 1965, senior photo.

Never Give Up

Marshall and Joyce at Dallas' New York City apartment.

CHAPTER 21

Although he had a number of other job offers, when Marshall graduated from the University of Michigan, he went back to work at Brookhaven National Laboratory as a developmental engineer.

By this time, Marshall's brother, Melvin, was in the Army. After graduating from high school, Melvin had gone to the State University of New York at Delhi, a two-year school similar to MVCC, where he studied hotel management. After graduation, he had worked for a year in New York City for Chock Full of Nuts, before joining the Army. He was now stationed in Germany. He was also married and the father of a baby girl.

Marshall was making a good salary at Brookhaven, so that Christmas, he sent Melvin's family to Germany so they could all be together. The

Never Give Up

following year Marshall himself went to Germany and spent the holidays with Melvin's family - which now included his new baby boy.

It was during his third year at Brookhaven that Marshall met a student who was doing an internship, similar to a co-op assignment, at Brookhaven. This intern would affect Marshall's life in a big way. Her name was Annie Cornelius. She was a student at Tougaloo College in Mississippi. Marshall and Annie became good friends. Then they fell in love.

Marshall's job was very exciting now. He had a lot more responsibility as a developmental engineer. After he had been working for a number of months, he began to notice others at Brookhaven who had even higher college degrees than he did. So he decided to start taking some of these higher level classes in night school, because he felt he needed to continue to learn and grow to be successful.

Many people he had worked with when he was a co-op draftsperson were now working for Marshall, who was like a junior engineer. Since he had worked as one of them, he related better to the group than the senior engineers. The draftspeople even told Marshall he was a better communicator! Now he could actually see the importance of all those English classes.

Marshall began to think about teaching. In a sense, he felt he was teaching the draftspeople already. Maybe he could teach a larger group - of students. He still enjoyed the research work but wanted to combine both. However, that would require a masters degree and a PhD!

Marshall had now been at Brookhaven National Laboratory for four years. They had just given him a big raise in pay. But two weeks later, he quit his job, took Annie, whom he had recently married, and registered for college once again, this time at the University of Massachusetts at Amherst.

Throughout college and his years at Brookhaven, Marshall and his mother Mildred had become much closer. She became his friend, and he often went to her to discuss his work and studies. She began to understand more about all the technical things her son was doing and so enjoyed listening to him. Finally, a time had come when they could form a really close connection with each other.

Marshall was well into his studies at the University of Massachusetts at Amherst when Mildred died tragically in a car crash.

Never Give Up

Marshall and Annie on their wedding day.

CHAPTER 22

Marshall spent five years at the University of Massachusetts at Amherst, where he was a B+ student. During this time, Marshall and Annie also became the proud parents of two sons, Alan and Kevin. He received his masters degree in mechanical engineering May 1972, and his PhD in August 1974. He was now *Dr.* Marshall Jones!

While at the university, part of Marshall's time had been spent as a teaching assistant. In his last year, he was advised to do more research work before teaching at a large university. So Marshall interviewed with many companies. In the end, he accepted a job as a mechanical engineer at GE's Research and Development Center in Schenectady, New York, where they had the latest research equipment and facilities.

Never Give Up

For the next eight years, he also taught evening classes in engineering and math at the Schenectady County Community College.

Today, Marshall continues to work for GE's Research and Development Center. He will soon celebrate his 25th anniversary with the company. He is still deeply involved in research, working with lasers and fiber optics, to find better, more efficient ways to make such things as medical equipment, light bulbs, and jet engines.

Marshall's work is known throughout the world. He has received 35 United States patents. He also has won many awards, including the national 1994 Black Engineer of the Year Award and the 1999 Pioneer of the Year Award. He still hopes to teach and do research at a university someday.

Although his job at GE keeps Marshall extremely busy, he always leaves time for his volunteer work. He is involved in many community activities, both locally and nationally.

One of the most important of these is his work with school children. He frequently visits schools to do a laser show and to talk about his life and his experiences. He explains to students how very important it is to get an education - and how important it is to never give up, whatever obstacles there may be.

Marshall Jones was not born wealthy. His mother and father were not there to raise him. He was raised by a loving extended family. He was not born a genius by any means. He had to work hard to do well. He had no "master plan." His future evolved bit by bit. He overcame many obstacles along the way. But he *never gave up.*

Today Marshall says, "I truly believe in my heart that anyone can achieve anything they want if they are motivated enough - and are willing to work hard - and are not afraid to fail sometimes." He advises students he visits to be patient and to work hard. He tells them, "If you don't try, you'll never know how much you can do."

And, to this day, he repeats the words Uncle Lawrence spoke long ago:

... Do the best you can in school.
Then you will be successful and have a good life.

*Dr. Marshall Jones giving acceptance speech for the
1994 Black Engineer of the Year Award
Baltimore, Maryland.*